In The Deep

Lloyd
Anesu
Ngongoni

Liquid Cat Publishing House
A Division of Liquid Cat Universal
Los Angeles, California

www.liquidcatbooks.com

ISBN: 9798846864917

Dedication

To everyone who moved on without a proper, genuine apology or closure you deserved,

CONGRATULATIONS.

If nobody told you, I am proud of you, that's not easy.

Just remember, no matter what you might have gone through, love will find you again.

*Regardless of your past or how many times you have been hurt, someone is going to find
you and love the person you are.*

*They will appreciate your scars,
All you have to do is believe!*

Prologue

You have probably heard a thousand stories about someone with a broken heart who eventually moves on and finds the right one, goes off to the Caribbean, and lives happily ever after. Well, these are stories about life, love and loss. Lessons I believe everyone comes to appreciate at certain points in our journey, and they specifically dwell on the aftermath that follows a breakup, moving on, healing, and that voyage towards self-rediscovery and reinventing ourselves.

It might be the end of a two-week fling, or dismissal of a sidepiece because the risk of getting caught by the 'main partner' or the betrothed is getting higher by the day. It may be that heartbreak that devastates you to the core, have you curled up in your bed, hugging your pillow sobbing, and slobbering until your head hurts. Playing that slideshow of memories you had created and the sudden realization that it was all gone. The type of heartbreak which drives some of the brightest of minds to suicide, the kind which only hits once. It is that mystifying, dreadful period of confusion, anxiety, and insecurities about yourself and the future.

These are followed by endless trips down memory lane, lethargy, laziness, and teary-eyed pleas to get back together. I didn't know how to move on, get on with my life again, no one ever taught me how to, but everyone expected me to do it.

It's no secret these days that the world has gone astray. Some would argue that the world is still the same, there's just less in it. Morals imparted to us by culture, religion and our parents have been disbanded, rather ignored in this millennial age, but that's a story for later. The good thing about the heart is that it adapts, it tries by all means to avoid the same horrific situation, but most of the time we choose to ignore the signals, our instincts, that gut feeling, or that tachycardiac rhythm when we are about to change the world or make the worst decision of your life. All these are nature's defense mechanisms, the body's anti-terror attack protocol but we ignore them. I don't blame us, we were never taught how to.

We have all been hurt, and l am not trying to compare pain, pain is pain but it is an undeniable fact that some people have had it far worse than others. The concept is still the same because ultimately the goal is to move on, accept the reality of our own story and proceed with our lives with no regrets because at some point what we lost was exactly what we wanted.

l have realized that love is more of the thorns than the shiny catchy roses which give us the beautiful fragrance and luminescence, more of the quarrels which happen behind the direct messages (DMs) than the to-die-for; love we post on our statuses and stories, more of the insecurities we are afraid to reflect on our partners than the maturity we try to portray but deep inside struggling with emotional trauma, dating Post Traumatic Stress Disorder (PTSD) which dates as old as our childhood. Less of the

MCMs (Man Crush Mondays) and WCWs (Woman Crush Wednesdays), more of the silly issues which go beyond midnight being solved.

More of the sacrifices than the actual gifts, the thoughtfulness than the actual price tag on the gift, more of the endless conflict between cultural ethics and modern-day dating etiquette, a ravaging battle between weaponized feminism and toxic masculinity rather than being each other's help, whatever that means with your person. More of lemons than oranges. Therefore, true love is more of blue than red and it is not entirely romanticism.

Love is not always easy and ego has no place. However, love has greater depth than the sorrowful parts for which I seem to have a fetish. Love also comes with the joys and successes you celebrate together and if you found the right partner, you will help each other reach your purpose. It is this love that has taught me how to care for others (solidifying the values I learnt from a Christian childhood) but most importantly to care for myself. One of my weaknesses is that I quickly get carried away, more often than not, I overextend myself, putting myself in situations that compromise me and what I want to achieve.

The only problem is that it quickens my fatigue in a relationship that I feel is one-sided, I easily feel drained and completely unmotivated to continue trying especially if you value reciprocity and your beloved 'boo' isn't meeting you halfway, which brings me to my next point. I used to believe in reciprocity, the fifty-fifty effort rule, perhaps it is there, somewhere. I slowly came to the revelation that relationships were highly variable; a 90 - 10 at one time, 70 - 30 at the other, and in the worst-case scenario 100 - 0.

What helped drive this point home was beautifully explained in karma; 'The love you give out will always come back to you. You just won't get it back from the people you expect or give out to most of the time'.

Take a moment to think about it. Just as there are people you love and don't love you back, there are people in your life that are investing in you, praying for all sorts of good things in your life, and simply loving you that you have forgotten about. Same as pain, I have hurt people (intentionally or unbeknownst to me) who have never hurt me in return, and I have been hurt by people whom I have never hurt before. It's the circle of love and pain and if you look at it at both ends that's karma in a nutshell.

The greatest gift love came with was purpose. My identity changed from my own to someone's own. Doing anything to see my person happy, despite the tow it took on me. This became my burden when that love was lost and with it went my purpose. It took me a while and probably ages to come. Reinventing, recalibrating, and recreating that bond with myself that I had lost chasing the wind because unless you truly understand and love yourself, you won't be able to completely love anyone.

Contradictory to popular opinion, I believe that in order to love, unconditionally; love should be a 3-way system (as illustrated below). True love has to go from me (being myself) to a higher power (God, in my case) and then to the other person, because the person to person relations, I mess them up all the time. I believe that when both parties serve a higher power, their purposes align with God and what they want out of life automatically aligns as they are facing the same direction.

Personally, love is still a mystery and I don't think I have even experienced half of it. Its vastness and abundance are beyond our understanding which is why this book is so special to me because in a way it's exposing me to the world and revealing all the fraudulence. I am neither an expert/guru on the topic of love nor have experienced more heartbreaks than anyone, I would like to think I was fortunate enough to have found world-whirling love at a young age.

So I write these poems, sometimes with a heavy heart, or worse with tears drenching my word pad and blurring my vision. Unfortunately, some lessons and breakthroughs come as an outcome of mishaps that may be relationship-threatening or relationship-ending, thus the mystery I was talking about. The level of uncertainty is beyond reason, we don't know if we have met the one already and let the chance slide, perhaps you are dating the one for you right now or you are yet to meet them.

I can't help but doubt our part in all this, probably it was meant to be, a game of chess and we are but just pawns. I have found solace in these pages and this ink, they bear the enormous emotional weight the shoulders can't. I hope that reading them might help other people let go and forgive, understand that it's okay to grieve over a break-up like a funeral because it is, and find comfort in knowing that you are not alone and you will be okay. One day you will look back and say, 'that was a messed up week, month(s), or year(s)', whatever the duration it takes you. Healing will come your way if you let it. Find peace in the remaining ruins which is life without the ones we love.

So if you ask me what love is, I probably won't give you a solid answer, but I will show you the manifestation of love in my daily life, and all these lessons which love has taught me. Maybe I don't know anything at all, maybe I am still trying to make sense of it all. I am just a paper tiger, an ink junkie; a man who writes about love but actually dreads and fears it, bearing the scars that only love can heal.

In a nutshell, these poems are pieces of my life, words I wish I had said when the time was right. It's a collection of gems, and experiences; good, bad, terrifying, and also motivating. It is in these pages I have buried my sanity and my soul. In a way, this is a book that saved my life, encrypted in these three chapters; Denial, In search of lost time, and Acceptance.

I hope that you may find your way to healing by going through these pages and realize that you are not alone. That seemingly incurable sadness will end and you will find your way back to yourself. And also, poetry doesn't have to rhyme, it just has to touch someone where your hands cannot, so I bleed on this paper because this is the only way I know how to let loose. How to not let these demons get the best of me. That's how I survive the storms.

TABLE OF CONTENTS

Un.

Denial

It is a defense mechanism, a shield, a barrier we cast to assist us in processing loss (Break up in this context) slowly so that we can cope with it.

"Denial is a shock absorber, of the soul. It protects us until we are equipped to cope with reality" - C. S Lewis.

Young Love

I have been on top of a mountain, right at the pinnacle,
And if you have too, you know the feeling,
To have the world at your feet, waiting on you to conquer
it.

That's how I felt with you by my side.
You were the light in my darkness, that flickering light at
the end of the tunnel,
Always reassuring me of better days ahead.
The summer warmth in the winter of my thoughts,
An oasis amidst the desert of my trying day,
My biggest supporter, my number one fan.

The first girl who stole my heart with nothing but simplicity
and utter realness, beauty, and
a strong God-fearing character.
It was this special person, I finally felt safe to take off
my social armour and show my truest
self.

At a very young age, I was swooped off my feet by love. Yes,
love.
Or so I thought.
The kind of love I wasn't scared to show the world.
In an era where relationships aren't meant to last long,
we defied the odds, learning and
growing together.

It is in growth that we grew apart, interests changed with
time ultimately leading to the
unprecedented future which was a devastating breakup.
All the promises and plans made and accomplished went
into the drain.

How we couldn't resolve our differences remains a mystery
but those were some of the best
years of my life, which flew past me like the winds of
August.

And I had just gotten a rude awakening.
Life teaching me that I can't have everything I want,
the way I planned it.
It was the kind of love that was not just good, it was great
and electrifying.

Baby Steps

Dark, gloomy nights never seemed to end.
An endless tunnel filled with misery and regret.
Four corners of his room witnessed it all, the fall of an
angel,
From glory into a bottomless pit of pain and sadness.
He even changed his playlist, trying to tame this madness,
Melancholic music was his lullaby,
Heart-warming memories of the love he lost were his alarm
but it was nothing apart from
an agonizing slap of reality,
That she was gone.

Drenched in tears, his pillow wept,
For it could no longer bear the sorrowful secrets it kept.
Oblivious to the real reason why she left,
He was relentless in search of answers she could not
present,
Or the lies he thought she wanted to protect.
They had created so many memories, so much magic that
she became ubiquitous,
omnipresent.
Every picture, every story, and even some of his favourite
sites reminded him of her.

Why, why, why?
The boy kept asking,
For he had experienced love that was breath-taking,
An illuminating connection,

To the greatest joys that life could give.
Perhaps he got so comfortable with what he had that he
couldn't notice the signs,
What he probably thought to be the endgame, was
probably the beginning of a cataclysmic
end.

Self-pity and resentment overtook his train of thought,
Along with feelings of unworthiness for he had past
transgressions, he never thought she
could forgive so the only logical explanation was karma.
Prayers upon prayers the boy kept sending to the Greatest
above,
That his lost love may return like a dove.

The Dark Side of the Moon

Who knew you had it in you?
Cause I certainly didn't see it coming.
How could I?
You gave me no reason to doubt your promises, let alone
your love.
I was so certain of where your heart belonged,
I could openly testify that it resided next to mine.
Your intentions were so pure, so raw that no light shined
any brighter.
Untamed passion.
Unquenchable desire.

How you changed from being sweet and kind to someone I
didn't recognise,
A stranger, rather a familiar stranger.
You unleashed that side of you that I only heard in the
stories you told me.
Victory tales of how you vanquished guys that now and
again asked you out.
It was this girl you had embodied,
Released into our little cocoon, the needle that busted our
bubble.

The proud yet humble,
Strong yet broken,
Savage yet caring,
And all the other traits which made up the undesirable you.

You turned a new leaf and began writing your story in a
whole different ink from the one we
used in ours.

It was these days I learnt to listen to my gut, my instincts,
For a week something wasn't right,
Something was off.
My whole body was screaming all kinds of warnings,
Needless to say, I never seemed to pay attention,

Red flags can seem maroon-ish when you are in love,
And besides,
I had your word and to me, that was enough.

I guess when it comes to matters of the heart, we all have
that one blind spot, and we all are
naïve in a way,
The downside of trying to see the best in everyone,
especially the ones you love,
It leaves you open, vulnerable to hurt, a certain kind of
pain only loved ones know how to
inflict.

Maybe we are designed to break, to teach us how much we
can take and still endure.
Maybe this is how the future survives the past,
How history always finds a way to repeat itself,
Days of the future past,
The ancient future.

It all happened so fast,

For a while, I thought you were going to come back running
into my arms.

And deep down I still do.
I played many scenarios in my head of how the lost lovers
would reunite,
Running, hugging, and kissing in the rain,
Some kind of fairy-tale.

Time flew by,
Days became weeks, months and before you know it, a
while grew into years.

Summer born winter,
And winter grew up into spring,
The family kept multiplying.
I understand how proud you were whenever I asked you
back into my life,
It was that 'I-made-it-without-you' kind of pride, not very
hard to pass,
Common among ex-lovers,

The desire to prove that you are much more than what
your partner thought you to be.

The necessity of the treatment you gave, I can't say it fitted
the diagnosis of my condition,

All I can say is you were a better person than that but you
probably needed it to keep on
moving.

I guess this is how you showed the world

that you moved on,

Or pretended to heal.

In My Dreams

'It's not like it used to be. Some days are good; the sun feels like healing on my skin and I don't call out your name in my sleep. But there are other days, where it feels like whatever it was that made me someone you could love, you took it with you. I guess I'm still learning to be the person you left me with.'
- Blake Auden

I knew the end was coming long before you left.
Now that you're gone, I only see you in my dreams.

In my dreams, I reminiscent of the old days,
Days you used to laugh at my jokes,
Days when all we had was each other and that was enough,
Days when distance wasn't a factor because we were riding the same wave and no tide
could push us off course.
I remember the days, I remember it just like yesterday.
Memories flood my mind, overriding my awareness, taking control of my consciousness,
I lose track of time in the conversations we used to have,
Plans for the future,
How we would have conquered the world,
Our version of Bonnie and Clyde,
Joker and the one Harley Quinn,
Too corny to be Romeo and Juliet.

In my dreams, I see you.
Maybe, it's because I miss you,

Or I never really got over you.
I have tried moving on, but no one ever seems to replace
you.
That's the thing, they were special in every way, every one
of them, but they just weren't
you.

It's just that the magic of someone new never lasts long
enough.
Somehow, we only want those we can't have.
It's those we lost or never knew we existed who leave their
mark,
The others barely echo, it's a sorry state of affairs.

The mind has a weird way of availing that which is hidden
from us,
Buried in our subconscious.
Like a phoenix from the ashes, you rise and hover above
the clouds of my thoughts.
Possessing my train of thought, steering it straight into the
subway of throwbacks,
memories, of what was.

To the days when this was enough for you;
When I felt like I could love you the way you needed.
To the days when I could offer you nothing but the words in
my throat, and you couldn't
remember how to love the monsters beneath my skin.
It was these days we lost each other.
It was these days you learned to let me go.
Perhaps that's how it feels, to be so close to paradise,

To be close to Heaven,
Because what l felt was truly a force greater than l.
Indeed, love has a smell, and to me it was yours.
So when l thought of moving on, washing your scent off my
jacket was a place to start.
"Perhaps it's because I am always trying to retrace my steps
back to a spot where I should
have jumped off the Ferryboat headed to the bank called
life without you, but ended up
dawdling on the wrong wharf or, with my luck, took the
wrong ferryboat altogether.

In my dreams, l feel you.
Like the early morning winter breeze,
Or the late-night summer winds,
You caress my whole,
Nerve by nerve, l feel every impulse, every transmission.
Gently palpating my anatomy from the cranium straight
down to my last phalange.
I touch your forehead with my palm, kiss it,
I let my fingertip touch your chin softly in a way a grown-up
touches a child's chin to prevent
it from crying,
I traverse your lower lip with my finger back and forth,
back and forth.
Euphoria these dreams are,
Waking up with a big smirk on my face which lasts for but a
moment,
Followed by the unavoidable post-mortems;
The lingering pretence of an attachment after we can't even
be touched by someone who

used to mean so much and lastly,
The realisation that much that once was can only happen in
my dreams.

"I want you to know, I would have pulled the ribs from
under my skin if I thought it would
make you smile; if it would show you I could still make
room in my chest."

In my dreams, l hear you whisper underneath your breath,
Prophesying your undying love for me,
Telling me how much different l was from the others,
And how impactful l had been as your lover,
Acknowledging all those traits you loved about me, along
with the monsters embedded in
my skin.

Rudo so (Oh Love).
I would smile at you as we lay there, breathing in each
moment, assimilating the sweet
words you would have spoken,
As if it was the first time those words escaped your lips,
That's the magic in saying things out loud,
It's not like I didn't know you loved me,
Vocal declarations just have a way of hitting a different
nerve.

I guess I don't know how to be anything other than
the person you left.

After All

After all these years, l still use the route we took from church,
I still replay the discussions we used to have,
The gossip, the music, and an eternity that had you and I painted all over it.
I still pass through the spot where we had our first kiss and plenty of others that followed,
How shy and completely innocent you were,
I visualise the whole scene,
Ripped straight from a Rom-com.
Snapping out of the reverie to the chirping sounds of the birds,
As though they are laughing at me,
At how much l am still hung over you,
The confusion,
Illusions,
Desperation.

I still read some of the letters you wrote me back in the day,
The ones that survived the fire,
Vengeance I took upon any of the things that reminded me of you,
And yes l still have some of them,
Blurred and washed out,
The-handle-with-care type of package.

Despite the ragged condition, the important part of the letter remains intact, those three

magical words,
Just the gesture,
If it wasn't the ride-or-die type of romance, I don't know
what is.

After all these years, I still get jitters when I receive your
text,
I am quite aware of what we have become,
But time and again, I wonder what we would have become,

If we had stayed en route to a place called us.
The oracle of the future said to listen to the past,
The mistake we keep making is that we search the past for
solutions,
For precedence to our present and possible future
problems but there are none.
Instead of answers, let us evaluate what our ancestors did
wrong, where we did wrong, and
ask for strength to do better, to be better;
Let us acknowledge where we triumphed against adversity,
Not looking at the how, but the why.
The reason behind the implementation of a certain
solution.
I guess I got side-tracked from all the lessons you taught
me,
But ultimately it is the growth we acquire from all this after.
I don't know if I will ever be the man I was with you,
Somehow, you did a better job at taming the beasts that
haunted me,
All I know is that they now roam free, devouring anything
in their path,

I stopped trying to cage them, the day you left.
They always had a soft spot for you.

After all these years, it's funny that l still talk to the moon
the way l used to whenever you
were away, and distance was testing us.
After all, truth be told, you were always better off without
me.

Easily Broken

I.

Life without you is not easy,
The grass isn't greener
And the path is not clearer.
The truth is I have been struggling with finding love in
other places.
Whenever I did, it was always in small traces,
Or unknowingly, I misplaced it.
I have lost tolerance over the years,
Probably due to the trauma I acquired over the years,
Or the victim mentality I think I have embraced.

That's the funny thing about pain,
Not that I go into places seeking it out or looking for new
ways to shutter this blood-pumping device,
But I have grown used to it.
I have gotten acclimatized to disappointment,
That and betraying, inherent parts of love.
Sometimes it's the fuel I need to write,
Other days it's the tamponade that weighs heavy on my
heart,
And others, I hold on to it like oxygen,
Something I am afraid to be without.

I have accepted the reality of things,
Of what we have become,
Undiscovered water I am still trying to navigate.

A darkness capable of snuffing out the faintest sign of light.
Live this way long enough and, eventually, the heartbreak
begins to feel comforting; like an
old friend.
If I'm honest, I can't help thinking it's the only thing I can
rely on not to leave.
It's the closest thing I have to home.

It's my prayer and salient hope that writing about it long
enough,
Will eventually cover these wounds with a fine layer of scar
tissue.

Something that resembles normality,
If not, then at least something close to it.
It's just a cold world out here,
And I am easily broken.
It is this game of hearts,
Where there are no winners or losers,
Just the broken, the sad,
The philosophers, the mad,
The regretful, the vengeful,
And all the other things that make love seem bad.
Is love that bad?
Or are we just bad,
In playing the game we make others wish they were dead.

II.

There's a hole in my chest,
An emptiness that sometimes scares me,
An abyss that longs for love,
For belonging.
Somedays I am better at taming it,
Keeping the shadows at bay,
Somedays I have no control.
It hovers over me like a saturated cloud waiting to release
the rain.
It feeds off my pain.
Nonetheless,
I am still here,
Arms open wide,
Hoping that maybe, just maybe, this time the verdict would
different than the ones before.

God knows, my intentions are pure,
If there's anything I am guilty of,
Is loving you a bit more than I should have.
Maybe I am just impatient,
But I don't think matters of the heart should take long to
decide,
So lately, I have been finding it a bit easier to run,
To flee,
To a place of solitude,
Because it's easier to walk away,
And I don't think I can take another cardiac fracture.

So go easy on me,

I am easily broken.

It took a while for me to get here,
I thought I could convince you to love me,
But slowly like a creeping storm,
I am beginning to understand that maybe you aren't meant
for me.

I am beginning to welcome the thought that maybe this is
not where I am meant to be.

With you, I am home, happy and safe,
I just wished you felt the same way.

Love Hurts

If I had the courage,
I would have packed a bag with your name on it,
Filled it to the brim with all your possessions,
T-shirts, jerseys, and all that reminded me of you,
But I had neither the courage nor an ounce of hope,
I burnt it all.

Nevertheless, I still found ashes of your belongings on my
skin,
Entangled within the strands of my hair,
The dirt in my fingernails.
Every time I saw any of it,
It was a painful reminder of days gone by,
Not what I had lost but the fact that at one point I was
exactly what you wanted.
Nothing lasts forever after all, except forever itself.

Love has a face,
To me, it was you.
A subtle line between pain and imprisonment,
I didn't know the difference,
It was all the same to me,
Two sides of the same coin,
The things we do for love.
A phrase we tell ourselves to avoid the inevitable,
To stall what is nigh.
Love hurts!

Deux.

In Search of Lost Time

I made the mistake of trying to move on quickly. I thought that maybe if I could erase your memories by making new ones with other people, perhaps the process would be less excruciating. Little did I know, it was a ticking time bomb waiting to explode.

You might be familiar with the phrase "If you do not heal what hurt you, you will bleed on the wrong people." No words could have truly explained what happened in my life at this stage. I met some pretty amazing humans in my quest for closure, but whenever things started to get serious, there you were, in the midst of my thoughts.

Unknowingly, your insecurities became my insecurities, your pettiness became my pettiness. And ultimately, they were reflected on the wrong people. These pieces are people who played an efficient role in my healing and my overall understanding of love.

Talking to the Moon

In that navy background plaited by a shiny, sparkling array
of stars, l lose myself.
Pondering what the future holds,
Will I ever find love again?
Or loneliness is the fate that awaits this black man.
Not just any type of love,
But the love that electrifies my senses,
Sanctify and illuminates my soul,
Fills my dreams with magic and gives me deja vu in the
morning.

Late in the night, l talk to the moon.
Like a surgeon examining a tuberculosis X-ray,
I get lost in that starry sky glamour,
I see your name in the stars,
Bedazzled in glitter and gold,
Shimmering among the constellation,
As if it was always there,
As if it was meant to be there.

I let my imagination run wild.
The longer I stare, the deeper l get lost within myself.
Flickering red-blue-green lights emanating,
From the Bluetooth sound device distantly guiding my
thoughts wherever that night's
journey may be.

She sees right through me,

Enticing me to open up whatever weighs me down.

Along with my two dogs, we share a glimpse of but a long
night.
It's funny because you were the one who got me into
talking to the moon,

Whenever you were away.
Now it's just one of those rituals that keep me sane.
The music doesn't give answers to questions I don't know
how to ask,
Rather it acts as a beacon, a guide, a compass.
Making me aware of my feelings and thoughts
It doesn't tell me what I want,
The moon and the music remind me that l may still be in
love, though l am no longer sure l
know what that means,
Being in love that is.

Yet l am glad that l have experienced love,
I no longer think of it the way other poets do.
It's not all soft and easy.
It's more grenade than a sonnet,
An explosive vest with a pressure trigger,
Controlled by your other half.

It is this journey, that the moon takes me,
Astutely masterminding the whole route.

It's these conversations in the dark that keep me in check,
Because the truth of the matter is,
I will be just talking to myself.

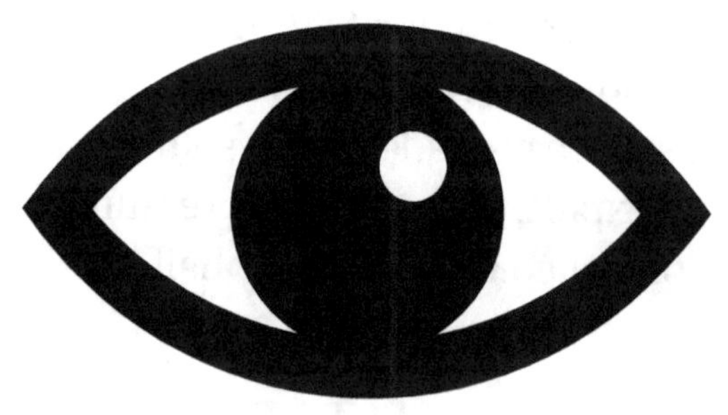

Love Contraband

I've found that some people find their way into your heart
over and over;

even if you don't

always want them to.
I think, in the end, it's because that's where
they're meant to be.

She is one of those people to me.
I can find peace in the knowledge that she's happy, and in
the end, that's all
I ever really
wanted.

She was a wild card, my wild card.
My kilo of cocaine, a bag of weed.
Something very rare, a jewel not many have seen.
My serenity, peace of mind, my happiness indeed.

Tough and strong outside but broken and vulnerable in
need,

So she was an egg you see,
my egg.

A violent lover who gave her heart away to a fool who
didn't appreciate it,

So along the way, the heart picked up scars, poignant
reminders of the past,
That she built up an emotional wall,
A safe place where she controls her life and dictates how
she lives it.

Never would she openly admit vulnerability,
Or conjure enough courage to face the demons that
haunted her head-on.
You would see her from time to time with rage in her eyes,
Perhaps she's waiting for the day she gets her revenge,
And scorch him in flames,
Then maybe she can forget.

But l knew what she needed.
How? You might ask.
It was pretty obvious to an observant eye,
Because for minutes l would stare at her,
Idle and smiling l would look at her,
Cursing the world for what it had done to her.
Praying so hard that l wouldn't encounter the idiot that had
traumatised her,
It would be reckoning for what he had done to her,
And other young ladies, for l, am certain he didn't stop
with her.

There was pain behind her every smile,
Inside tears masked by her every laugh,
A prisoner inside her mind, a mourning soul yearning for
freedom.

Our love was the forbidden type of love,
Fantasy kind of love, her favourite kind of fairy tale
romance,
Like a wolf that had found her mate, she seemed peaceful
for the moments l was with her.
Perhaps l am exaggerating my place in her life but l would
like to think that what we had
was special, magical.

A love story meant for the darkness to witness.

Many memories created, but three days stood out,
Amidst the winter weather, she was my midnight caller.
Like contraband, she would smuggle into my welcoming
bed,
Leaving me high, drunk, and addicted to her touch, love,
and smell.
Yearning for just a quick fix.
So she was my intoxicant, you see.

My warmth in the night,
whispers in the wind.
My shelter.

Invisible to the world,
She was one of those secrets untold,
A jewel, a gem, a diamond.
Lettuce, carrots,
cabbage, and mayonnaise,
a perfect salad.

A black queen,
Royalty,
Her majesty.

Mars and the Moon

Not everything I write ends up as a poem.
Sometimes, the words are more exhale than poetry,
More acceptance than regret,
More surrender than anything else.
No matter how hard I try, I can't always bend the ink into
something worthy of what we were,
at least not like a real writer would.

Even if I could, I'm not sure it would help;
I guess some days poetry is the stitches,
Other days it's the wound.

I am Mars and you are my Moon,
Distant, but close from afar.
On the rarest of days, we show ourselves to the world,
Young, dumb and stupid, we take on the world,
In search of our niche in the world,
But dark is the world, and not everything that glitters is
gold,
In the darkest of times, we bask in the splendour of your
moonlight.

I am Mars and you are my Moon.
Your brightness overshadows my imperfections,
You make me want to do better,
I am a better person with you.

Solely, l am a sinner,
Together, we are still sinners but trying to do better,
Guiding each other to doors of confession.
Like a moon, each of us have a few facets known to the
earth, to everyone but never its full
sphere.

Most of us never meet those who understand our full
rounded self.
So, I show people only that sliver of me I think they'll grasp.
I show others slices and so do you.
But there's always a facet of darkness I kept to myself,
Myths about extra-terrestrial lifeforms until l met you.

Alone you are beautiful,
Together we are a sight to behold,
I am Mars and you are my Moon
I want to read every book you've read, hear the music you
love,
Go back to the places you know and see the world with
your eyes,
Learn everything you cherish and start a life with you.

I am Mars and you are my moon
In a constellation of many, l shine brighter beside you,
Neither shaken by your glorious glow,

Nor anxious of what the future holds
But confident that in you, l have found my one.

I wanted to think you don't know me,

You can't.
But oddly you do.
I am not too proud to say when lm wrong and maybe l was
wrong about you
And also l was wrong about me.

Maybe l don't need to shutdown forever,
Closing my heart like an out of business book store,
Maybe l don't need to run away so fast
I am Mars and you are my moon.
Some poetry is stitches,
Other days it's the wound.

Coldplay

Thinking of you is not uncommon to me,
It's never uncharted territory,
Rather familiar grounds,
A place of frequent visitation where the last seen can date
to as early as a few moments ago,
As the ink graces this paper I find myself smiling,
Because all this writing, is trying to you out of me.
Most of the time, the journey is involuntary, the mind
wanders on its own.

I keep wondering where I went wrong with you;
Perhaps it was the patience I lacked,
Or the inability to assess situations in your shoes, I don't
know.
Probably my overly simplified view of the world and how
your big issues seemed petite to
me.

You rekindled the flame in my heart that had burned out a
while back,
My spirit had found purpose again and this time it was to
help you find your way back to yourself.
However, an introvert and pessimist you were,
A combination of toxic negativity and uncertainty,
A portion I tried to counter with positivity, optimism and
hope.

I wanted to be your knight in shining armour,
I know right (the cliché), but I wanted to be that for you.
Make you see life on the positive side.

Hard to please and even harder to converse with,
Comparison and complaining were your daily bread,
You fed these cancers of the mind,
They festered.
They spread.

What I don't understand from the life of me is;
How I cared for you when nobody else did,
How I saw the light in you when all hope was lost,
How I tried to change your life while no one else was
willing to believe in you,
How I tried to save you at the risk of losing myself,
swimming the deep waters.
And how I gave and gave and gave.

That's why it hurts.
That's why every little thing bothers me the way it does.
I feel too much.
I let people get the best of me.
I always give them more than they deserve.
I loved you. You probably loved me too, in your own way.
And still, you ran me over.
You gave me darkness when all I did was give you light.
All I ever wanted was for you to see me, as I saw you.

Roses are red,
Violets are blue,

No matter how hard it gets,
I hope I never get as cold as you.

It Always Ends in Tears

I.

I try so hard not to entertain these negative thoughts,
Take the win and leave,
But regret is a strong feeling, if not among the strongest,
That' why graveyards receive more flowers than the living,
I am not sure if that is what l was feeling,
Regret,
Probably a pinch of betrayal coupled with a vibe of being
used.
Talk of surprises, this came straight from the blue,
Camouflaged,
A chameleon on steroids,
It caught me unaware and unprepared.

I knew what we had was impossible,
But l thought it was worth fighting for.
Initially, this was your jam,
Your favourite song,
On repeat every night,
Gradually the song became redundant, a dud,
A broken record,
Did l really mean something to you?
A thought to self,
Or was l just a by-product of lust and loneliness?
Did l mistaken lust for love?
Roses for actual thorns?

As much as you weren't mine,
You were mine as much.

I get it though,
Sneaking around isn't good enough,
Not for me, not for you, not for anyone.
And logically you did the right thing,
You found someone you could love openly,
Without fear or shame,
Was l just a placeholder? Still l wonder.

Reality just caught up with me faster than l imagined.
You made me feel like I was special,
Different from the others,
I should have known you were a player,
The first time you treated me like trash.
I do have a tendency of trying to see the best in people,
Which makes me ignorant to red flags, signs.

You fooled me once,
You fooled me twice,
Now I am just the fool, you enjoy fooling around.
I just wish you could have told me yourself,
It's sad, how you loved me at your convenience,
Gave me pieces and portions,
Phrases and notions,
While l gave you myself, whole;
Compliments and conversations,
More often at my own expense.

You probably had your reasons,
Even so, l am bitter, battered and bruised,

Scarred from the love, l never had,
From the person who never was mine,
Be that as it may, l wish you well.
This game of hearts isn't for the faint hearted.

II.

Pride will always be the longest distance between two
people,
Time and again humans have proven this to be true.
I thought we were moving towards the right direction,
Building a foundation to our own fairytale,
But Alas,
The wolf came a tad early,
Huffed he did,
Puffed he did also and eventually the house succumbed
and he blew it away.

I don't know what I thought,
I wanted to believe what we had was something worth
fighting for,
That's where I make the mistake most of the time,
I overextend myself,
I guess it's the dire need for validation that we all have,
The desire to be enough that we all crave.
Now I just count the days as the time flies,

Nostalgic of your smile and how you used to make me
laugh.

Who was I trying to fool?
A girl like you was never meant for a guy like me,
In other words, I am just saying you were way out of my
league,
And I was just a young dumb boy who had a dream.
In some ways, I guess you knew that,
Maybe I am just being insecure,
Or lashing out,
Or simply just in denial.

Whatever your reasons were, for entertaining me that is,
Thank you,
For a while, you were the dream I went to bed early for.
We were good together,
I just wish you had seen that,
I just wish I didn't have to convince you.

Sometimes it makes me sad,
You being gone,
I have to remind myself that some birds aren't meant to be
caged,
Their feathers are just too bright and majestic,
And when they fly away,
That part of you that knew it was a sin to cage them up
does rejoice.

After all has been said and done, I just wanted to love you.
To show you that love can be a beautiful thing if you let it.

But the more I tried to love you, the more I pushed you
away.

Inadvertently the seeds of love I sowed gave birth to the
weeds that sprouted and
overwhelmed the harvest.

It is my prayer that with time, you may be open to love,
that you may find someone who
puts your heart at ease, a safe haven to unpack what has
been holding you back.

And hopefully, you may find someone to call home.
And that's it.

Like a Sunflower You Are

You got diamonds in your skin,
No wonder why you shine bright in the glamorous sunlight.
It's as if we are hit by different wavelengths of radiation
from the same sun.

Your skin just has a way of isolating the good properties,
giving you that glow that shines so
bright even in the darkest of days,
Like the sunflower you are.

Call it human evolution,
You are just on top of the food chain.
Coupled with your smile,
Unwavering faith and positivity,
You radiate happiness.
Warm and inviting as the sweet summer sun,
So you shine, and shine bright you do,
A glistening glow of YELLOW,
And GREEN by default,
Let your vibrant petals stretch out to the sun,
So that the world may enjoy your beauty,
Like the sunflower you are.

In your moments of doubt and uncertainty when you don't
know what to do,
When you are in a dark place, when it seems like you are
being buried,
All you need is that change of philosophy,

Perhaps you are planted,

BLOOM

Remember you're a sunflower and follow the sun,
follow the light
And also don't forget,
the teacher is always silent during the test,
Be positive,
Like the sunflower you are.

Stalker You Made

The heart only wants what it wants, and for a while,
mine only wanted one thing,
YOU!
And it had been a minute since it wanted anything else
until I met you, minding your own
business in the library.
From the day I started talking to you,
I couldn't get enough of you.

Constantly checking my phone,
Hoping to just see your text.
I went to bed thinking of you,
Woke up thinking of you.

Spending my days in a trance,
Thinking of how it would be spending quality time with
you.

But I guess that, we will never know,
On your hierarchy of priorities, I am but below,
Tried to get your attention, tried to make you look my way,
Nothing I do seems to steal your focus.
Nobody is really busy they say, just a matter of priorities,
which is true.

If only I could climb up the list of relevancy,
Get your attention frequently,
I wouldn't pass up this opportunity.

Time and again I check your online status, I see you.
Wondering who it is you're talking to.

As distressing as it is I lurk around our 4-5 messaged chat
like the stalker I am,
Reading those texts we had,
Marveling at how great a conversationalist you are,
Rather a great conversationalist you seem to be,
But suddenly saddened at the disproportionate state of
affairs, I have huddled myself in.

Reciprocity is dead,
Or maybe it's still early in this cocoon of ours to assume
that.

Replying after two days or even more,
And when you do eventually reply,
The texting ratio is five to one.
That's my curse, I get carried away far too quickly,
My overzealous nature is too prominent to hide,
A hopeless romantic I am,
"She is playing hard to get," I convince myself,
trying to motivate the quitter in me.
"If she is amazing, she won't be easy," I keep telling myself.

After a while, it became boring,
The warrior in me laid down his sword,
The soldier ran out of magazines.

"Too early," the Romeo in me muttered.
"Keep your foot on the pedal,"

"I am tired fam, tired," I respond.

It's that self-preservation instinct kicking in with a pinch of
self-respect and a tad bit of
pride.

"Enough is enough, mate."
Well, at least you tried.

Trois.

Acceptance

"Happiness can only exist in acceptance." - George Orwell

"Acceptance is tomorrow, even if the pain is still there, you realise it may always be and somehow, that's okay."
- Brianna West

"Acceptance makes an incredible fertile soil for the seeds of change." - Steve Maraboli

Letting you go was probably the hardest and most loving thing I have ever done and I don't know if I have enough courage to do it again.

"Maybe one day, we will meet again and explain to each other
what really happened. Maybe one day we will finally
understand. Until then, I hope you live your best life and I
hope you really do all the things you always wanted to do."

- R.M Drake

Dear Mary Jane

I.

There is something about the rain that tingles my subconscious, awakening my dormant thoughts. Like a bolt of lightning jolting through my whole being, l become aware of every sensation. It's like a light switch which l have no control over, but whenever it goes on, everything comes to light.

However, rain just has a way of getting to me, to everyone, l would like to think. It's probably that artistic connection poets and nature share. I have been thinking about you lately my darling Mary Jane, wondering where you have been and with whom. Will I ever see you again, brush my hands through your well-conditioned weave, or knotty, kinky and curly hair, it really doesn't matter.

The sweet smell of your cologne filling my nostrils right down to my lungs, leaving a faint resonance of your scent on my t-shirt whenever you hug me. Been constantly replaying about our last encounter and how the events played out. I am sorry l let my ego get in the way of what was good, l should have listened to what you had to say before I got all emotional and stormed out.

I know you loved me in your own way, probably the best you could or rather knew how to, it just wasn't enough for me. As unfair as it sounds, deep down, l felt like you could have done more to nurture our bond, our relationship. Towards the end, loving you was like trying to hold water in my hands; fruitless efforts, like trying to breathe through lungfuls of salt.

But that was as much my fault as it was yours. I think we were both trying to swim against the tide, or maybe we were the tide; bearers to our own demise. Understanding the role I played in our destruction has been hard to come to terms with, a tough pill to swallow, and I want you to know that I'm deeply sorry. I hope you still feel like there's a way of loving that doesn't end up taking everything from you.

That you can hold whoever he might be, without his edges cutting into your skin. Perhaps it's the trauma from your past relationships, wounds left by those long gone that you found it hard to love or the absence of a reliable male figure in your life that made you build walls and doubt the intentions of men, my intentions. It was my hope and plan that someday we would trod across the boulevards of famous cities and towns we only heard in movies.

It was one of the long term goals, celebrating how far we had come and how we had finally made it. I guess what I am trying to say is take me back to the good times, where we could walk in the rain like nobody's business, gossip and talk about how other couples aspired to be a version of us.

The reality of things is that l am not that guy anymore and definitely you are not that girl anymore. Be that as it may, you will always be a part of me, a shadow that persists even in the dark, scars that tell a story of what was there before, now dead, sandcastles washed away by the tides, ship wreckage washed up on the shore.

After all has been said and done, l am ready to love again my darling MJ because I have hope that love will find me again, and hope is a good thing and good things never die. Until we meet again, it's goodbye. For now.

II.

My darling Mary Jane, it's me again.
Since you, I have known no peace,
And my heart no sleep.

I have been a pain killer for too long that I no longer know
what's normal if presented to me.
Scars and bruises from people whom I confused as lovers
and most of all, myself.
I betrayed myself you see,
The man I wanted to be or at least saw myself as,
Morally upright and all.
But life is not black and white as I have come to appreciate,
I have become attracted to toxicity, handicapped
relationships that only take.
I have acquainted with it, like close friend.

It was my philosophy that maybe if I gave more, they would
eventually reciprocate and give more as well,
But that was a misconception and quite frankly \
naive on my part.

As life unfolded, I think I became toxic as well,
I became the things that I once despised and I can feel my
angels mourning as I ride with the
centaurs of hell.

I don't know if I will ever be that man again,
I don't know if I will ever recover from this,
But what I know is that I want to break the cycle.
I no longer want to be a victim of my own demise,
I no longer want to be an enemy of my own progress,
I no longer want to be ruled by emotion disregarding the
logic.

I no longer want to play hide and seek with emotions
wondering who will fall first or playing
defense wondering when is the good time run.
I no longer want to chase for love, because the thrill of the
hunt only lasts for a while,
I want to stay where I am wanted,
I want to love without fear of being too much or shame of
too vulnerable,
Because in the end, all we want is someone who
understands us,

Who is kind enough to notice the hell we've been through
and why we are this broken.
Someone who sees through our banters and adult
tantrums, an act just to hide our
insecurities and post-dating trauma.
Not with judgmental and spiteful eyes, but eyes that
comprehend why we behave the way
we do.
Someone who makes us feel comfortable with ourselves,
yet striving to do better,
to be
better.

And that's it.

No Longer a Slave of Fear

Pain has a way of lurching on to our lives.
It can be the fuel that motivates us,
But often, it feeds off our weakest moments and it becomes
the ocean that drowns us.

Everyone has a story, and everyone is working through
stuff.

Let your scars be part of you,
A living memento that you have loved,
And you will love again,
Because you can build an altar from bones:
Let your knees kiss the pavement and call it worship.

Because heartbreak can be a god,
If you fear it enough.

It Takes Two to Tango

I don't blame you,
I want you to know, nothing that happened between us was
your fault.

The only thing you were guilty of was trying to love me;
even when we both knew how hard
that would be.

If you took anything from me, it's because I offered it
willingly. Every inch you took was an
inch I gave.

You don't owe me anything, after all I just wanted you to be
happy and if that meant leaving
me to find it then that's okay with me.

If it was meant to be, it would be simply that.

Light in the Ruins

We must trust that the Lord will not only put us on the right path but that He will also give us the strength to walk it.

It wasn't until later, that I realised, maybe these experiences aren't meant to be traumatic but self-actualization processes, Journeys toward self-discovery, for it is in the darkest of times we discover our true nature and maybe my role in her story had come to end.

I have made peace with that and I am ready to move on.

Sometimes fate forces us to face the situations we least expect and most dread, it is in how we choose to respond that differentiates us.

Emotional Toddler

Slowly I am learning,
To let go,
To be without,
To be enough,
For myself.
I am learning not to clip my own wings,
Downplay my worth,
Not to deny myself the love I know I deserve.

I am learning to accept the reality of things,
Not a very a strong suit of mine,
But still I am learning.
The wounds hurt a little less,
And the scars are beginning to feel like art engraved on my
skin.

I am beginning to appreciate the beauty that comes with
being without,
And meditating on the lessons that made you want out.
I am getting old but stuck in my old ways,
I want to grow but growth takes time,
I want healing,
But it's a slippery slope.
I struggle sometimes.

I have lost count of how many times I texted you and never
got the courage to press the
send button,

How many times I rehearsed a phone call or just showing
up on your door step.
Pride was never a limiting factor, fear of rejection was,
Because I knew the answer was going to be as same as
before.

I thought if I tried hard enough,
You would see how serious I was, how much you meant to
me,
And how much I was willing to sacrifice to get you back.
Unknowingly, these were parts of me I kept giving
regardless of the ill-treatment you kept
dishing out.
I guess I was just scared of being alone,
After all these years,
That made me want to hold on to a fading dream.

I am learning to fill the void with hobbies I had forgotten I
liked,
Rekindling talents I had forgotten I possessed,
And also trying other new things.
Slowly, I am learning and understanding that good things
meant for me will come my way,
Even if things don't go well,
I rest easy in faith and belief,
That someday what is mine will boomerang its way to me,
Because hope is the only way.
I age by the day but emotionally,
I am just a toddler making baby steps.
So, slowly I am learning to walk away from what isn't meant
for me.

Moving On...

Healing is a strange little thing. Very delicate in nature, all it takes is a relic of the past to drag you back to square one. You might be okay and doing well for weeks, and just that one song movie, or scent takes you back and before you know it, you are right back where you started. Some days, I feel like Mozart reincarnated, rhythm and melodies finding their way to this ink, hitting all the relevant notes. Some days, I just feel normal, inconspicuous, incompetent, and invisible. It's as if the world would benefit from my non-existence and it is these days I reassure myself that no matter how bleak the road may be, I will get through it.

The complexity of this matter is beyond my years and well beyond the human mind, but l have managed to pick up a few pointers, and cookies which might assist you in finding peace. Lower your expectations because happiness and expectation are sworn enemies that never see eye to eye. Be positive and have faith because mindset is important. It influences us, in ways we cannot even begin to imagine. I don't think we ever really move on, that we are at a specific point free from our past. In some ways, evolution occurs emotionally as well. We learn not to let the past hurt us in ways it used to.

I believe moving on may be voluntary or a state of acceptance that is forced upon us by reality. Voluntary being evoked by early acceptance and the desire to change one's current circumstances. It comes as a realisation that this pain is not going away until certain changes are made hence the birth of acceptance. It may be an acquired state of emotional numbness and fatigue.

If one is unfortunate and acceptance does not come easy and quick, one tries, by all means, to fight for what he/she has lost. This continuous process coupled with continual rejection due to the repeated trying to get back together eventually forces one to accept what is and try to move on. I think the problem is we are afraid to let go. To be without. We are afraid of what might happen, of what would come next. Hence, we self-sabotage ourselves thinking that maybe if we try hard enough, they will change. That if we try hard enough, they will come back, and inadvertently we are telling ourselves that we are the problem, that we are not enough.

I think that is the problem with a lot of people in hard, broken relationships. They are afraid to move on because they are too insecure about the future. Sadly, this is the story for many of us, we feel trapped. We are afraid to initiate that conversation because we don't want to destabilise things. We feel caged within the walls of fear, that we, ourselves create. That is why some of us stay. That is why some of us deal with it because the devil you know is better. We learn to live with the pain, the trauma, and the abuse. We do not know how to be alone anymore.

Sometimes we just don't know how to put ourselves first. Moving on requires guts because it's not as simple as social media and movies perceive. It is different for everyone and has no particular formula, just like grieving, it has no blueprint, some have it hard than others - it is a fact, and it's completely normal.

That is the variation of life influenced by our background, upbringing, and our philosophy of life, our general overview of life as a whole. Thus, the process has no deadline or period, take as much time as you need as long as you are preparing yourself, and taking those baby steps forward.

New Beginnings

I have chased ghosts - phantoms, figures of my imagination. Feelings I thought I had, love I thought I had found. My battery ran out, I am tired, fatigued. It's hard chasing what you cannot see, worse off looking for something that doesn't want to be found.

If these experiences have taught me anything, it's that I will never be ready for whatever life throws at me. I won't ever be adequately prepared. Right words will fail me when it counts. There will be moments when my faith will be tested, put on trial, in both good and bad times. I have learned I can go on waiting for something sustained by hope and nothing more, or I can put it aside and shrug my shoulders. It's not easy being hopeful, it requires a certain level of dedication, patience and an enormous amount of sheer will. Hope is a good thing and good things never die, therefore we should not lose hope, come what may.

Let it be that flickering light that guides us through the dark times, the promise of a better tomorrow. I bravely accepted the fact that I can't keep my heart safe anymore than I can stop love from taking everything from me. I have come to accept that people are going to leave our lives at certain points in time. Though we may not have control over how it happens, we do however, have control over how we choose to react to the situation.

Contrary to this thought, I have also figured that heartbreak is cancer that can slowly eat you up, metastasising to other relationships in your life if you do not face the feelings head -on. Some feelings just can't go away by closing your eyes, you just have to let yourself feel the pain and like a phoenix from the ashes, you rise and move on.

We can't break down every time someone leaves, but this doesn't come easy. How we react and respond is a demonstration of how much control we have over our awareness. So in a nutshell, it's important to:

Respect your time, space and sanity, aggressively.

Respect all of these things, knowing when it's time to free yourself from dead, toxic and traumatising family relationships, intimate relationships, friendships and work environments

I have learned to stop saying yes when I don't mean it - to live as authentically as I know how. Knowing that I am not perfect, but the best I can do is be real. To be patient, knowing that there are great things in store for me, unwavering faith in the unpleasantness of whatever my current situation maybe. And as long as I remember to keep my eyes fixed on the light, it is well with my soul. So as one door opens, another closes, I will move forward with the knowledge that unlike so many others, I have another second, minute, hour, day, week , month or year ahead of me - another shot at making it all the way around sun, and a chance to get it right this time around.

Where your mind goes, your energy flows (the law of attraction/ vibrations) - speak good things unto your life and the universe will reply likewise so meditate on those positive vibes, and the universe will repay its debt like a Lannister.

So here's to:
New beginnings
Blank pages
Clean slates
Reboots
Fresh starts

Another chance to be better than we were yesterday. Instead of waiting for a new year to improve and work on yourself and how you relate with others - you can start today, now, all you need is to make that decision and stick with it. Instead of making New Year changes, let's make life changes!

Less talk more action
More doing and giving
More motivation and positivity
More compassion

Let's be present, put our phones down and enjoy the time we get with our loved ones.

So as I lay my pen with these dying words:
May your heart find peace in this cruel world.
Though the road may be dark and you can't see,
Just know that healing is not far as people make it seem.
Maybe not today or tomorrow,

Lloyd Anesu Ngongoni

Acknowledgements

My deepest gratitude goes to my parents for being the pillars that give me strength. For trusting and having faith in whatever I try to do. You are my role models. To a few individuals; namely Precious Ruzande and Melborne Nyamadzawo, your constructive criticism has been nothing but appreciated. It is through your input that these words are worthy of being among the shelves with other things called books.

Jakob and the team at Liquid Cat Publishers, thank you for believing in me, in this book. You have brought my thoughts to life, and hopefully they will resonate with others in the world. Your hard work and support is irreplaceable. Thank you for giving me a platform to change the world, with these words.

To Blake Auden, my favourite poet, even though you don't know me, your words gave me strength to write mine. Your ability to be so vulnerable and untameably raw, is what I aspire to achieve. It is through your art, that I found myself wanting to be an artist too.

To my friends and followers on social media, this book is for you. Lastly, I would like to thank God. *Caha mihi vires* (My strength is from Heaven).

About the Author

Lloyd Anesu Ngongoni is from Chitungwiza, Harare in Zimbabwe. He is a mental health advocate and an animal lover, currently in his final year studying Veterinary Science at the University of Zimbabwe. He is also a taekwondo athlete and has a deep passion for poetry. Poetry for him started as a way of venting, saying what he was feeling in a raw, uncensored way. "In the Deep" is his first collection of poetry published by Liquid Cat Books.

You can find more from Lloyd Anesu Ngongoni here:
Instagram: @anesu_open_meditation
Facebook: Anesu Open Meditation
Website: www.anesuopenmeditation.wordpress.com

Join the conversation! Post pictures reading the book, or your favourite quotes and experiences related to this book on social media using #inthedeepbook #anesuopenmeditation #lloydangongonipoetry #liquidcatbook and you could be featured on our official instagram and Facebook pages!

About the Publisher

At Liquid Cat Publishing, we work with our writers every step of the way on their literary journey, helping to bring out the most from their work. From an idea and rough draft, to editing and publication, Liquid Cat Publishing helps our authors produce high quality, interesting and entertaining books.

Our books frequently appear on the best-sellers lists and our authors are among some of the best known in their genre. At Liquid Cat Publishing, we believe that every author has a story to tell, and that every story deserves to be told.

You can order our unique and thrilling books direct from us on our website, www.liquidcatbooks.com or find them featured on Amazon.

Want more Liquid Cat? Find us on social media!

Instagram: @Liquidcatbooks
Facebook: Liquid Cat Books
Twitter: @liquidcatbooks